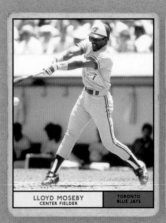

LLOYD MOSEBY
CENTER FIELDER

TORONTO
BLUE JAYS

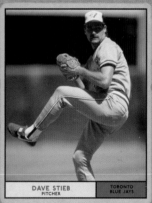

DAVE STIEB
PITCHER

TORONTO
BLUE JAYS

THE STORY OF THE TORONTO BLUE JAYS

Published by Creative Education
P.O. Box 227, Mankato, Minnesota 56002
Creative Education is an imprint of The Creative Company
www.thecreativecompany.us

Design and production by Blue Design
Art direction by Rita Marshall
Printed by Corporate Graphics in the United States of America

Photographs by Getty Images (Abelimages, Bernstein Associates, Lisa Blumenfeld, John Capella/Sports Imagery, Jonathan Daniel/Allsport, Diamond Images, Otto Greule Jr., Otto Greule/Allsport, Tom G. Lynn/Time & Life Pictures, Brad Mangin/MLB Photos, Jim McIsaac, MLB Photos, Redroom Studios, John Reid/MLB Photos, John Reid III/MLB Photos, Charles Ruppmann/NY Daily News Archive, Dave Sandford, Rob Skeoch/MLB Photos, Larry W. Smith, Chuck Solomon/Sports Illustrated, Rick Stewart, Rick Stewart/Allsport, George Tiedemann/Sports Illustrated, Ron Vesely/MLB Photos)

Library of Congress Cataloging-in-Publication Data

LeBoutillier, Nate.
The story of the Toronto Blue Jays / by Nate LeBoutillier.
p. cm. — (Baseball: the great American game)
Includes index.
Summary: The history of the Toronto Blue Jays professional baseball team from its inaugural 1977 season to today, spotlighting the team's greatest players and most memorable moments.
ISBN 978-1-60818-059-2
1. Toronto Blue Jays (Baseball team)—History—Juvenile literature. I. Title. II. Series.

GV875.T67L43 2011
796.357'6409713541—dc22   2010025479

CPSIA: 110310 PO1381

First Edition
9 8 7 6 5 4 3 2 1

Page 3: Pitcher Jimmy Key
Page 4: Center fielder Vernon Wells

BASEBALL: THE GREAT AMERICAN GAME

THE STORY OF THE TORONTO BLUE JAYS

Nate LeBoutillier

CREATIVE EDUCATION

CONTENTS

NORTH OF THE BORDER

How exactly Toronto, Ontario, got its name is a subject of debate. Before European settlers made their way to the place that is now known as Toronto, various native tribes lived in the area. Some people contend that the Mohawk word *tkaronto* (which means "where there are trees standing in the water") is the origin of the name, while others point to the Huron word *toronton* ("a place of meetings") as the source. Regardless, Toronto has carried its name since 1834, and today it supports a population of more than 2.5 million inhabitants, nearly half of which were born outside of Canada.

As Canada's largest city, Toronto is an important cultural center with a cosmopolitan reputation, and as such, it's no surprise that the city attracted its share of professional sports teams during the 20th century. In 1976, Major League Baseball voted to expand its number of clubs and granted Toronto a franchise. The team was placed in the American League (AL) and named the Blue Jays to keep with the blue color scheme of such other Toronto sports franchises as the defunct

As home to the 1,815-foot-tall CN Tower (pictured, right edge), Toronto can lay claim to the tallest building in North America.

PITCHER · DAVE STIEB

A fierce competitor who hailed from sunny California, Dave Stieb was a key cog in Toronto's pitching rotation in 1979, contributing eight wins that year. By 1982, he was a star, posting a 17–14 record by way of some hard inside pitching and a wicked "dead fish" curveball. On September 2, 1990, Stieb claimed no-hit fame by completely shutting down the Cleveland Indians 3–0 in nine innings. Known for his glowering gaze—which was sometimes directed at teammates who made mistakes or umpires who were stingy with strike calls—Stieb, who accrued 10 double-digit-win seasons, is widely regarded as the best pitcher in Jays history.

DAVE STIEB
PITCHER

TORONTO
BLUE JAYS

STATS

Blue Jays seasons: 1979–92, 1998

Height: 6-foot-1

Weight: 195

- **7-time All-Star**
- **30 career shutouts**
- **176–137 career record**
- **1,669 career strikeouts**

Huskies of the National Basketball Association, the Maple Leafs of the National Hockey League, and the Argonauts of the Canadian Football League.

For their inaugural manager, the Blue Jays chose Roy Hartsfield, a former player and minor-league manager who had distinguished himself in the Brooklyn/Los Angeles Dodgers organization. The team then put its first roster together via draft selections and player signings. Catcher Phil Roof became the first player in Blue Jays franchise history when he signed a contract, and the team acquired another catcher, Alan Ashby, as one of its marquee signings soon after.

Exhibition Stadium, a multipurpose venue that had hosted Argonauts football games since 1959, was chosen as the Blue Jays' home. Although the stadium had been the setting of many championship football games, it was less than ideal for baseball. The stadium had been built next to Lake Ontario, which meant it could experience very cool temperatures and other problems, such as an overabundance of pesky seagulls. Nonetheless, excitement levels were high in Toronto, though Hartsfield stayed realistic about his team's chances for success in its

The 1977 Blue Jays started well at 5–2 but struggled after that, losing 11 straight games late in the year.

inaugural season. "Anyone who tells himself he can win a pennant with an expansion team is just spitting into a gale," he told reporters.

The Blue Jays played their first game against the Chicago White Sox on April 7, 1977, at Exhibition Stadium. Almost 45,000 Toronto fans braved icy winds, flurries, and below-freezing temperatures to cheer on their new team. The Blue Jays fought off the cold—and the White Sox—to deliver a 9–5 victory. Even though subsequent wins were few, fans continued to flock to home games in record numbers throughout the season.

The young club ended up in the AL Eastern Division cellar in its first three seasons, losing 107, 102, and 109 games, respectively. Still, there were highlights worth applauding. On September 10, 1977, at Yankee Stadium, third baseman Roy Howell drove in nine runs with five hits, helping the Jays smoke the mighty New York Yankees 19–3. And shortstop Alfredo Griffin did the team proud in 1979 when he collected 179 hits, 10 triples, and 81 runs to earn AL co-Rookie of the Year honors. Toronto had some building blocks in place.

ALFREDO GRIFFIN

Alfredo Griffin showed a shaky glove early in his career, leading all AL shortstops in fielding errors in 1979, 1980, 1981, and 1982. Still, his steady hitting and scrappy play made him an All-Star by the 1984 season.

OPENING DAY

On April 7, 1977, the expansion Toronto Blue Jays were getting ready to play their very first game at home against the Chicago White Sox. A bitter wind blowing off Lake Ontario swirled springtime snow devils and brought temperatures inside Toronto's Exhibition Stadium to a frigid -10 degrees. "I was in the clubhouse, and we looked out and said, 'No way, we aren't playing this one,'" Jays first baseman Doug Ault recalled. "I was thinking it was so cold there was no way we were going to play. And then there were 44,000 people in the stands, and I thought there was no way we *wouldn't* play." And play they did. After the Sox scored two runs in the top of the first inning, the rookie Ault answered by clobbering the first long ball in franchise history off Chicago pitcher Ken Brett, warming up the mass of chilled Jays fans in attendance. Ault homered again in the third inning, this time a two-run shot that tied the score 4–4. The Blue Jays went on to win 9–5, and Ault's heroics tied a major-league record for the most home runs in an opening-day game.

CATCHER · PAT BORDERS

Pat Borders was never a superstar, but he was a player known for remaining cool under pressure, a team cornerstone, a rugged defender of home plate, and a reliable hitter. Borders's greatest highlight might have been the 1992 World Series, when he batted .450 to help the Jays win their first world title and was named World Series Most Valuable Player (MVP). He left Toronto as a free agent in 1995 and bounced around to eight different teams before announcing his retirement in May 2006. Borders won an Olympic gold medal in 2000 as a member of the United States' baseball team.

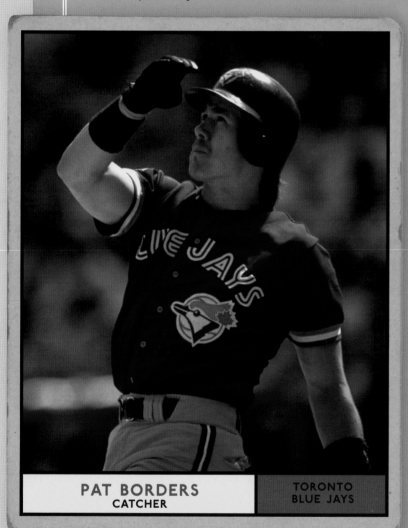

PAT BORDERS
CATCHER

TORONTO
BLUE JAYS

STATS

Blue Jays seasons: 1988–94, 1999

Height: 6-foot-2

Weight: 200

• **1992 World Series MVP**

• **346 career RBI**

• **Career-high 30 doubles in 1993**

• **.988 career fielding percentage**

FIRST BASEMAN · CARLOS DELGADO

A herculean Puerto Rican who signed with the Jays as a 16-year-old in 1988, Carlos Delgado took almost eight years to mature as a ballplayer. The years of work paid off, as he became one of baseball's most dangerous sluggers—a hitter who rarely missed a pitch when he was ahead in the count. A classic home run hitter who could drive the ball with power anywhere between the foul lines, the personable Delgado was also the Blue Jays' team captain. His patience at the plate was a never-ending source of frustration for opposing pitchers and brought his batting average to a career-high .344 in 2000.

CARLOS DELGADO
FIRST BASEMAN

TORONTO
BLUE JAYS

STATS

Blue Jays seasons: 1993–2004

Height: 6-foot-3

Weight: 240

- **2-time All-Star**

- **473 career HR**

- **1,512 career RBI**

- **22-game hitting streak (2000)**

PUSHING FOR A PENNANT

he Blue Jays steadily improved throughout the early 1980s, and the fine individual performances continued. Fiery pitcher Dave Stieb, whose "brushback" pitch often whistled near batters' heads, added sizzle to Toronto's pitching rotation, and second baseman Damaso Garcia turned frequent double plays with Griffin. The bats of right fielder Jesse Barfield and first baseman Willie Upshaw also began to heat up in 1982, as the pair combined for 39 homers.

In 1983, center fielder Lloyd Moseby, who had earned the nickname "The Shaker" during his days as an Oakland high school basketball player because of his razzle-dazzle moves, became the first Blue Jays player ever to score 100 runs in a season. The club took much of its leadership that season from Stieb, who won 17 games and struck out 187 batters with an impressive combination of fastballs and wicked curveballs. "Just watching a great pitcher like him pitch rubs off on everyone on the team," said Toronto catcher Buck Martinez.

The Blue Jays ended the 1983 season above .500 for the first time in team history, posting an 89–73 record and finishing fourth in the AL East. After the team jumped to second place in 1984 under new manager Bobby Cox, it seemed the Jays were ready to soar.

Toronto ran roughshod over the AL East in 1985, winning its first division championship with a 99–62 record. The title put the Jays in their first AL Championship Series (ALCS), where they were pitted against the AL West champion Kansas City Royals. The Jays started out strong, building a three-games-to-one lead in the series, but then their hitting and pitching fell apart, and they lost the final three games and the series. The dejected Jays went home empty-handed as the Royals went on to win the World Series.

Toronto took a step backward in its 10th season, as many of its pitchers struggled. Only rookie relief pitcher Mark Eichhorn, noted for his unusual sidearm throwing style and wily breaking ball, showed much pizzazz. The youngster won 14 games on the season and posted a club-record 1.72 earned run average (ERA).

While Toronto's pitching misfired in 1986, its offense came to life in a big way. Shortstop Tony Fernandez—nicknamed "Mr. Gadget" due to

TONY FERNANDEZ

Tony Fernandez suited up for seven different major-league teams in all but spent
the bulk of his career in Toronto. He gained renown for his sure defense—
especially his ability to make backhanded stops and leaping throws to first.

SECOND BASEMAN · ROBERTO ALOMAR

The youngest son of big-league second baseman Sandy Alomar, the fiery Roberto broke in with the San Diego Padres in 1988 by mimicking his father's switch-hitting ability at the plate and athleticism at second base. He joined Toronto in 1991, and on May 10 of that year, against the White Sox, he became 1 of only 55 players ever to hit home runs from both sides of the plate in the same game, a feat he accomplished 4 more times in his career. He made headlines during Toronto's 1993 World Series win by batting .480, stealing four bases, and collecting six RBI.

ROBERTO ALOMAR
SECOND BASEMAN

TORONTO
BLUE JAYS

STATS

Blue Jays seasons: 1991–95

Height: 6 feet

Weight: 190

• 10-time Gold Glove winner

• 210 career HR

• .300 career BA

• Baseball Hall of Fame inductee (2011)

the fact that he created his own workout equipment from random items such as wedges, putty, and ball bearings—spanked a club-record 213 hits and posted a .310 average. Barfield led the AL with 40 home runs, and left fielder George Bell slugged 31 of his own. Still, the Jays' 86–76 record left them out of the playoffs.

In 1987, Toronto posted the second-best record in the major leagues at 96–66, and Bell won the AL MVP award by hammering 47 homers and driving in 134 runs. Unfortunately, the team played in the same division as the 98–64 Detroit Tigers, and a seven-game losing streak at the end of the season cost the Jays the AL East title and the playoff berth that went with it.

A slow start in 1988 left the Blue Jays 11 and a half games behind in the division race by mid-July. Although they rallied to post the AL East's best second-half record with 45 wins, the Jays ended the season in third place. "The baseball season is a marathon," said Toronto manager Jimy Williams. "It takes a lot of heart and perseverance. You have to take adversity and bounce back. You've got to bust your butt for nine innings, whether the score is 10–2 or 2–1."

TERRIFIC 10s

The number 10 has twice been a significant number in record-breaking Blue Jays performances. On September 14, 1987, the Blue Jays walloped 10 home runs in a single game to set the major-league record for most homers in a game by a single team. In an 18–3 win versus the Baltimore Orioles in Toronto's Exhibition Stadium, catcher Ernie Whitt bopped three dingers and left fielder George Bell and shortstop Rance Mulliniks jacked two apiece, while teammates Fred McGriff, Lloyd Moseby, and Rob Ducey hit one home run each. On September 4, 1992, the number 10 again took center stage as the Blue Jays racked up an amazing 10 hits in a row versus the Minnesota Twins. In the bottom of the second inning with one out and the Twins up 3–0, Kelly Gruber eked out an infield single. Pat Borders and Manuel Lee followed with singles before Devon White doubled, Roberto Alomar singled, and Joe Carter tripled. Minnesota then made a pitching change, after which Dave Winfield singled (but was thrown out at second), John Olerud singled, Candy Maldonado tripled, and Gruber doubled before Borders made the inning's final out and left the Blue Jays with a 7–3 lead.

DAVE WINFIELD

When Toronto started the 1989 season 12–24, Williams was fired, and the team's hitting coach, Clarence "Cito" Gaston, was promoted to manager. A close friend of baseball legend Hank Aaron, Gaston had 10 years of experience as a big-league outfielder, having spent his best seasons with the San Diego Padres. Gaston brought a more personable managerial style to Toronto, refusing to hold clubhouse "chew-out meetings" and instead discussing player troubles one-on-one. "One thing I did learn as a player," Gaston said, "is that a manager should try to be honest with the team. If he is going to make a change, he should talk to the players involved. I respect the players, and I hope they respect me."

Gaston's respectful leadership style seemed to work, as the Jays went 77–49 the rest of the season and won the AL East crown before losing to the eventual world champion Oakland Athletics four games to one in the ALCS. Although the Jays slipped to second place in 1990, nearly 4 million fans made their way to Toronto's new indoor ballpark, SkyDome, breaking the major-league single-season attendance record.

THIRD BASEMAN · KELLY GRUBER

Gruber made a name for himself by earning a spot on the 1989 All-Star team. That season, he also received a shiny tricycle, compliments of his teammates, after he hit for the rare cycle (a single, double, triple, and homer in the same game) in April. The star third baseman— whose mother, a former Miss Texas, had sung with the likes of Elvis Presley and Kenny Rogers—made baseball music by blasting 31 home runs and collecting a whopping 118 RBI the next year. As a capper to his final season with the Blue Jays, he hit a key home run in Game 3 of the 1992 World Series.

KELLY GRUBER
THIRD BASEMAN

TORONTO
BLUE JAYS

STATS

Blue Jays seasons: 1984–92

Height: 6 feet

Weight: 185

- **2-time All-Star**

- **117 career HR**

- **443 career RBI**

- **1990 Gold Glove winner**

JOHN OLERUD

FLIRTING WITH .400

When Ted Williams of the Boston Red Sox batted .406 in 1941, the occasion marked the last time a major-leaguer finished a season hitting .400 or better. In 1993, a member of the Blue Jays—first baseman John Olerud—made a serious run at that hallowed number. Olerud hit over .400 in his first two seasons of college ball at Washington State University but suffered a brain aneurism before his junior season. He survived the scary incident and played one last college season before being drafted by the Blue Jays. Without ever playing minor-league ball, Olerud joined the Jays in 1989. By 1993, Olerud had fully adjusted to the major leagues and carried a .402 average into August. "I'm more aggressive early in the count," Olerud said of his hitting philosophy. "When I was in college, I'd wait and get deep in the count. But it's not the same [in the majors]. I'd get behind in the count and pitchers would peck at the corners. Everybody has a strikeout pitch." Olerud cooled off late in the season but still finished with a nifty .363 average and won the AL batting title—a first for any Toronto hitter.

FALL CLASSIC COUPS

I n late 1990, the Blue Jays made a change that altered the face of the franchise, sending Fernandez and first baseman Fred McGriff to the Padres in exchange for slugging outfielder Joe Carter and versatile second baseman Roberto Alomar. The additions helped Toronto win the AL East again in 1991, but the team then lost to the Minnesota Twins in the ALCS. The Blue Jays' painful runner-up status was again underscored as they watched the Twins go on to win the World Series.

In 1992, the Blue Jays assembled their most impressive collection of talent yet. Among the new additions were fiery pitcher Jack Morris, who had hurled a 10-inning, complete-game shutout for the Twins in Game 7 of the 1991 World Series; pitcher David Cone, known as much for his mischievous personality as his lethal split-finger pitch; and towering right fielder Dave Winfield, a 12-time All-Star and

JACK MORRIS

7-time Gold Glove winner. These veterans, along with steady catcher Pat Borders and hot-hitting first baseman John Olerud, helped Toronto vault to another AL East title with a 96–66 record.

The Blue Jays met the Athletics in the ALCS. Oakland won Game 1, but Toronto bounced back to win Games 2, 3, and 4, with a two-run homer by Alomar in the ninth inning of Game 4 helping propel the Jays to a 7–6 victory. After Oakland won the fifth game, the series went back to SkyDome. Toronto left fielder Candy Maldonado went deep in the third inning of Game 6, helping the Jays earn a 9–2 victory and clinch the Canadian franchise's first World Series appearance.

The first international "Fall Classic" pitted the Blue Jays against the Atlanta Braves. The Jays dropped Game 1 but came back to win Game 2 when power-hitting third baseman Ed Sprague bopped a home run in the ninth inning. The Jays then won Games 3 and 4 before the Braves rebounded to capture Game 5. A nail-biting Game 6 saw Winfield smack an 11th-inning double to give the Jays a 2–1 lead. And in the bottom of the 11th, Jays pitcher Mike Timlin saved the game—and triggered a wild infield celebration—by charging a bunt by Braves outfielder Otis Nixon

ROBERTO ALOMAR

Over the course of his 17-year career, Blue Jays fan favorite Roberto Alomar set numerous major-league records for second basemen, including most consecutive All-Star Game appearances (12) and most Gold Glove awards (10).

SHORTSTOP · TONY FERNANDEZ

Fernandez, a native of the Dominican Republic, signed with the Blue Jays as a teenager. A skinny switch hitter with a skewed, wobbly batting stance that made it look like the bat was too heavy, Fernandez was a dependable hitter from both sides of the plate. In 1986, he posted 213 hits, a feat that broke a century-long, major-league record for most hits by a shortstop. Playing 2,158 games in his big-league career, Fernandez credited his durability to his collection of homemade workout contraptions. He left Toronto in 1990 but returned for three more brief stints in the years that followed.

TONY FERNANDEZ
SHORTSTOP

TORONTO
BLUE JAYS

STATS

Blue Jays seasons: 1983–90, 1993, 1998–99, 2001

Height: 6-foot-2

Weight: 175

- **4-time Gold Glove winner**

- **844 career RBI**

- **5-time All-Star**

- **.288 career BA**

and hurling it to first for the final out. The Blue Jays had made history, becoming the first team based outside of the United States to win a World Series. "I've dreamed about this more times than I've gotten out of bed," Timlin said. "I sat in class and dreamed about it. I thought about it all the time."

The highflying Jays wasted no time in making player changes to bolster their lineup even further. Eleven new players joined the club before the start of the 1993 season, including designated hitter Paul Molitor and hard-throwing hurler Dave Stewart. Toronto went 49–40 in the first half of the season and put seven players on the All-Star team, which was managed by Cito Gaston. With the midseason addition of blazing-fast outfielder Rickey Henderson, the star-studded Jays soared to a 95–67 record, capturing the division for the third year in a row. Toronto then won the ALCS, securing another World Series berth by topping the White Sox in six games.

Opposing the Blue Jays in the 1993 World Series were the Philadelphia Phillies, a team that had finished in sixth place in its division the year before. The Phillies proved a worthy foe by clipping

LEFT FIELDER · GEORGE BELL

In his first 4 full years with Toronto, the hot-tempered Bell averaged 31 homers and 104 RBI a season. He set team records by getting 69 extra-base hits in 1984 and clubbing 47 home runs (with a league-leading 134 RBI) in 1987. Bell, whose surly attitude got him thrown out of numerous games and won him few friends around the league, hit a walk-off home run in a 7–5 victory over the White Sox in the last game ever played at Toronto's Exhibition Stadium on May 28, 1989. He followed that up eight days later by homering in the team's first game at SkyDome.

GEORGE BELL
LEFT FIELDER

TORONTO
BLUE JAYS

STATS

Blue Jays seasons: 1981–90

Height: 6-foot-1

Weight: 190

• 1987 AL MVP

• 3-time All Star

• 265 career HR

• 1,002 career RBI

HISTORIC HIGHS

Game 4 of the 1993 World Series between the Toronto Blue Jays and Philadelphia Phillies lasted 4 hours and 14 minutes, taking its place in the record books as the longest World Series game ever played. The cumulative run count of 29 in the Blue Jays' 15–14 victory also set a World Series record for the most runs scored. Philadelphia outfielder Milt Thompson set the tone for the game early by ripping a three-run triple in the first inning. Phillies catcher Darren Daulton's two-run homer in the fifth broke a 7–7 tie, and outfielder Lenny Dykstra capped the inning with a two-run homer—his third of the series— to give the Phillies a commanding 12–7 lead. With the Jays trailing 14–9 after the seventh inning, Toronto, led by first baseman John Olerud, designated hitter Paul Molitor, and second baseman Roberto Alomar, pounded the Phillies' pitchers for six more runs and the win. "It was just one of those nights," said Jays shortstop Tony Fernandez. "If you were a hitter, you just hit everything." The scoring derby, although overtaken in the record books by a 2005 World Series game, will forever be a World Series classic.

BLUE JAYS

the Blue Jays' wings with wins in Games 2 and 5. Philadelphia nearly won Game 4 as well, jumping ahead 14–9 before the Blue Jays soared back in the 4-hour, 14-minute game to win 15–14. "It's always great to come back in that kind of ballgame," said Fernandez. "At one point, it looked like they had the game, but we just kept chipping away."

In Game 6 at SkyDome, the Jays held a commanding 5–1 lead until the seventh inning, when the Phillies pounded out five runs to grab a 6–5 advantage. But Carter came through for the Jays in the bottom of the ninth by hammering a one-out, three-run, walk-off homer to clinch the series. Toronto fans in SkyDome roared, and fans in the city danced in the streets as Carter stomped on home plate to give the Blue Jays their second world championship, their first at home. "We've got a team of All-Stars," beamed Carter.

Joe Carter (above) ended the 1993 World Series with only the second championship-clinching walk-off home run in World Series history.

LOSING ALTITUDE

Blue Jays fans were hopeful for a "three-peat" in 1994, but the team plummeted in the standings, posting a meager 55–60 record by the time a players' strike ended the season in August. The franchise continued its downward spiral in 1995, claiming only 56 wins and finishing in the AL East cellar for the first time since 1981.

The club began its 20th year by unveiling its "Level of Excellence," Toronto's version of a team hall of fame, and making George Bell and Dave Stieb its first inductees. Another player garnering accolades in 1996 was pitcher Pat Hentgen, who went 20–10 with a 3.22 ERA and 177 strikeouts to bring home the prestigious Cy Young Award as the league's best pitcher. "I didn't even think I'd make it through the season if you asked me in the middle of the season, when my elbow was killing me," Hentgen said. "I feel honored that my name's next to that award forever."

Also starring during that 1996 season were pitcher Juan Guzman, who led the AL with a 2.93 ERA, and Ed Sprague, who hammered 36

CENTER FIELDER · LLOYD MOSEBY

Lloyd Moseby made his major-league debut on May 24, 1980, when he was just 20 years old. Gifted with speed, a magnetic glove, and a strong arm, Moseby added his talents to those of Jesse Barfield and George Bell to create one of the best outfield trios in the history of the game. Moseby scored 104 runs in 1983 and ran up a 21-game hitting streak that same year. Before leaving Toronto in 1989, he stamped his name all over the Blue Jays' record books with such career totals as 255 stolen bases and 451 extra-base hits.

LLOYD MOSEBY
CENTER FIELDER

TORONTO
BLUE JAYS

STATS

Blue Jays seasons: 1980–89

Height: 6-foot-3

Weight: 200

• **1984 co-AL leader in triples (15)**

• **1986 All-Star**

• **737 career RBI**

• **.984 career fielding percentage**

home runs. Despite these impressive performances, the Blue Jays ended their anniversary season a disappointing 74–88.

In an effort to add grit and experience to their roster, the Blue Jays acquired several veteran players in 1997 and 1998, including star pitcher Roger "The Rocket" Clemens and muscle-bound outfielder Jose Canseco. Both acquisitions earned their pay, as Canseco crushed 46 home runs in 1998, and Clemens earned the fourth and fifth Cy Young Awards of his career in 1997 and 1998. In 1999, Toronto made another notable addition, hiring Jim Fregosi as its new manager.

Despite the added star power, the Blue Jays continued to lose altitude in 1999, 2000, and 2001, as their win total declined each year. Yet there was at least one bright spot: gregarious and powerful first baseman Carlos Delgado. In 2000, Delgado hit .344, blasted 41 home runs, and drove in a whopping 137 runs. "Being more mature helps a lot," said Delgado, who had struggled with impatience at the plate early in his career. "I am not swinging at so many bad pitches. I am still aggressive, but in the past I thought I could hit everything." Even Delgado's heroics were not enough to make Toronto a contender, and Fregosi was fired after just two seasons.

The 2002 Blue Jays opened the season just 17–33 before rebounding to finish 78–84, thanks largely to breakout seasons by several rookies.

ROY HALLADAY

Big right-handed pitcher Roy Halladay turned on the heat and emerged as a star by going 19–7; designated hitter Josh Phelps was named AL Rookie of the Month in August after hitting 7 homers and driving in 30 runs in just 28 games; and power-hitting third baseman Eric Hinske jacked 24 home runs and was named AL Rookie of the Year.

Halladay continued to throw fire in 2003. The 6-foot-6 hurler pitched the Blue Jays out of a 10–18 April slump, sparking them to a club-record 21–8 May and a 15-game winning streak in June. The team even notched

A SICK DAY TO REMEMBER

On September 26, 2003, Blue Jays first baseman Carlos Delgado was not feeling well. But the muscleman with the megawatt smile didn't call in sick. Instead, he suited up for that day's game against Tampa Bay and made the record books. In the first inning versus Devil Rays pitcher Jorge Sosa, Delgado hit a home run blast that clunked off the side of Windows restaurant in SkyDome's center field. The 3-run dinger marked the 300th homer of Delgado's career and added him to an elite list of 97 other players who had reached the triple century mark. Delgado blasted a solo shot in the fourth inning to increase Toronto's lead to 4–1. In his third plate appearance in the sixth inning, Delgado jacked another solo homer off pitcher Joe Kennedy to tie the game 6–6. With the Toronto crowd on its feet for his fourth at bat, Delgado spanked a long drive over the center-field fence, making him 1 of only 15 major-league players ever to smash 4 round-trippers in a single game. "I was pretty fired up. I'm not going to lie to you," Delgado said of the four long balls, which helped the Blue Jays secure a 10–8 win. "I was on cloud nine out there."

RIGHT FIELDER · JESSE BARFIELD

An exceptional outfielder with a rifle of an arm, Jesse Barfield led the AL in assists from 1985 to 1987 and captured the Gold Glove award in both 1986 and 1987. No slouch at the plate, either, the always-smiling Barfield became the first Blue Jays player to pinch-hit a grand slam (in 1982) and bang 20 homers and steal 20 bases in the same season (in 1985). His unmistakable batting stance—which featured a jutting left elbow and an upright bat—also facilitated 9 triples in 1985 and a whopping 40 round-trippers in 1986.

STATS

Blue Jays seasons: 1981–89

Height: 6-foot-1

Weight: 205

- **1986 All-Star**

- **2-time Gold Glove winner**

- **241 career HR**

- **716 career RBI**

JESSE BARFIELD
RIGHT FIELDER

TORONTO
BLUE JAYS

MANAGER · CITO GASTON

A talkative Texan with baseball in his blood, Clarence "Cito" Gaston became the first African American manager in the major leagues to win a World Series. He joined the big leagues in 1967 as a center fielder with the Atlanta Braves and played for the San Diego Padres from 1969 to 1974 before returning to the Braves from 1975 to 1978. He took over as Toronto's hitting coach in 1982, a position he kept until he was promoted to manager in 1989. With Gaston in command, the Jays won division crowns in four of his first five years and back-to-back World Series championships.

STATS

Blue Jays seasons as manager:
   1989–97; 2008–10

Managerial record: 894–837

World Series championships:
   1992, 1993

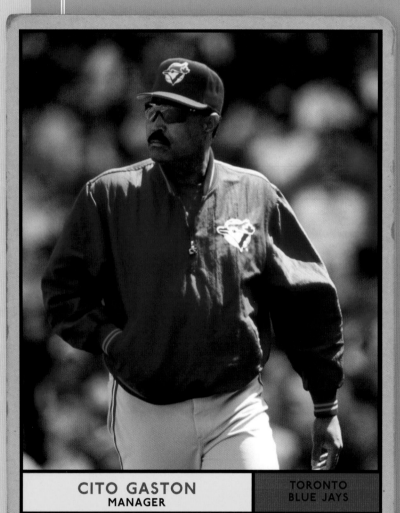

CITO GASTON
MANAGER

TORONTO
BLUE JAYS

its first-ever four-game sweep of the Yankees at Yankee Stadium in May. By the end of that 86–76 season, Halladay's baffling assortment of fastballs and curveballs had earned him a 22–7 record and the Cy Young Award. "It was an unbelievable ride for me," he said. "There were some games in there where I got a lot of help from my teammates."

CITO'S RETURN

n 2004, the Blue Jays took the field sporting new uniforms. A new logo depicted a fiercer-looking blue jay, and the team hoped to add more ferocity to its play as it challenged AL East kingpins New York and Boston. Unfortunately, 2004 turned out dismal as Toronto finished a miserable 67–94, the worst record it had posted since 1980. The biggest problem was injury, as Halladay, Delgado, and valuable outfielders Vernon Wells and Frank Catalanatto all missed time with ailments.

Injuries played a huge role in undermining Toronto's 2005 season, too, but the 2006 Jays showed signs of life. The team finished a respectable 87–75, 10 games behind the Yankees, and 5 Jays players—Halladay, Wells, third baseman Troy Glaus, shortstop Alexis Rios, and closer B. J. Ryan—made the AL All-Star team. In 2007, Toronto slipped to 83–79, though veteran designated hitter Frank Thomas made some history by notching his 500th career home run in his lone season in a Blue Jays uniform.

The 2008 season started out wretchedly enough that team management fired manager John Gibbons in June and re-hired Cito Gaston as the club's skipper. The move paid immediate dividends as the Jays clobbered the Cincinnati Reds, 14–1, in Gaston's first home game after his return. The fans repeatedly chanted Gaston's name, causing a commotion that brought up memories of Toronto's golden seasons in the early '90s. "It gives you goosebumps," said Gaston of his positive reception. "I'd really like to say thanks to all the fans for the way they treat me in this city, and tonight was a special night for me, and it's just great to be back. I just hope we can put some more games up like that."

The Blue Jays finished the 2008 season 51–37 under Gaston, but that was good enough for only fourth place in the ever-competitive AL East. In

VERSATILE VENUE

Toronto is one of the northernmost cities to claim a major league baseball team. The weather there is unpredictable, especially in the early spring, when snow is common. Such a fickle climate helped give birth to SkyDome (which was renamed Rogers Centre in 2005). This innovative ballpark, featuring a weather-conquering, retractable domed roof, opened on June 3, 1989. Weighing about 11,000 tons, the roof system featured 1 stationary panel and 3 that could move, stack, and tuck closed or slide open in 20 minutes. When closed, the roof sealed out blustery weather; when opened, it offered an outdoor ballpark feel. SkyDome's open roof also sometimes fueled a feisty downdraft that could foil hitters trying to slug home runs. A ground rule stated that if a game began with the roof closed, it must stay closed for the entire game, even if the weather cleared. Fans could stay at the Renaissance Hotel in rooms that overlooked the playing field and eat at many restaurants within the building, including a Hard Rock Café. The venue also contained a health club and mini-golf course, and a 110-foot-wide JumboTron video screen in center field magnified game replays.

BLUE JAYS

Jose Bautista shocked the big leagues in 2010. A relative unknown coming into the season, he slugged an AL-best 54 home runs with 124 RBI.

JOSE BAUTISTA

AARON HILL

The Jays clubbed a major-league-high 257 home runs in 2010, with Aaron Hill (opposite) hitting 26 and Adam Lind (below) slamming 23.

ADAM LIND

2009, the Jays struggled mightily, falling to 75–87. Worse yet, fearing that it would be unable to re-sign Halladay to a new contract, Toronto traded away its ace at season's end. Still, Toronto received a number of intriguing prospects in return, particularly second baseman Aaron Hill and sweet-hitting designated hitter Adam Lind. With Gaston at the helm for one final season, Hill, Lind, Wells, and slugging right fielder Jose Bautista battered the ball in 2010, while hurler Ricky Romero had a fine season on the mound. Toronto went 85–77 yet came up short of the playoffs.

Since 1977, Toronto has been a great place to meet for baseball. As a franchise known for its stellar leadership and perennially sound personnel decisions, the Blue Jays have become a team that can never be counted out—not even in the always loaded AL East. After celebrating two World Series titles in the 1990s, Toronto fans—and all of Canada—eagerly await the Blue Jays' next flight into championship territory.

INDEX